Happy Birthday Maddison
Love from
Grandma and Grandpa
Sept 8, 2004

UNDER THE MICROSCOPE

FORESTS

John Woodward

Gareth Stevens Publishing
MILWAUKEE

For a free color catalog describing Gareth Stevens Publishing's list of high-quality books and multimedia programs, call 1-800-542-2595 (USA) or 1-800-461-9120 (Canada). Gareth Stevens Publishing's Fax: (414) 225-0377. See our catalog, too, on the World Wide Web: http://gsinc.com

Library of Congress Cataloging-in-Publication Data

Woodward, John, 1954-
    Forests / by John Woodward.
      p. cm. – (Under the microscope)
    Summary: Presents the capsules that cast hundreds of tiny fern spores into the wind, an ivy leaf's delicate network of veins, and many more microscopic marvels.
    Includes index.
    ISBN 0-8368-1599-8 (lib. bdg.)
    1. Forest plants–Juvenile literature. 2. Forest animals–Juvenile literature.
3. Microscopy–Juvenile literature. [1. Forest plants. 2. Forest animals.]
I. Title. II. Series.
QK938.F6W64   1997
574.909'52–dc20   96-34489

First published in North America in 1997 by
Gareth Stevens Publishing
1555 North RiverCenter Drive, Suite 201
Milwaukee, WI 53212 USA

© 1997 Brown Packaging Partworks Ltd., 255-257 Liverpool Road, London, England, N1 1LX. Text by John Woodward. All photos supplied by the Science Photo Library, except page 29: Bruce Coleman Ltd. Additional end matter © 1997 by Gareth Stevens, Inc.

Printed in the United States of America

1 2 3 4 5 6 7 8 9 01 00 99 98 97

CONTENTS

ROOT SHOOTS

The soil beneath a forest of pine trees is often very poor in quality. Rainwater drains through the soil quickly, washing away the rich plant foods. The roots of a pine tree may have to probe deeply to find the water and minerals it needs. As the roots travel, they are fed by sugar that passes down them through a series of thin tubes. These tubes lie alongside what are known as xylem vessels that carry water and minerals up into the tree. The young roots are thin-skinned, at first, in order to soak up water. In time, they grow tough enough to anchor the growing tree.

The xylem vessels in this root, stained *blue*, form five bundles that run along the entire length of the root. They link up with similar bundles in the stem.

DIGGING DEEP

- If you were to find a hole in a pine forest, notice that the soil forms definite bands with a grayish, barren zone just beneath the surface. This is where plant foods have been washed away, forcing the tree to send its roots deeper into the ground.

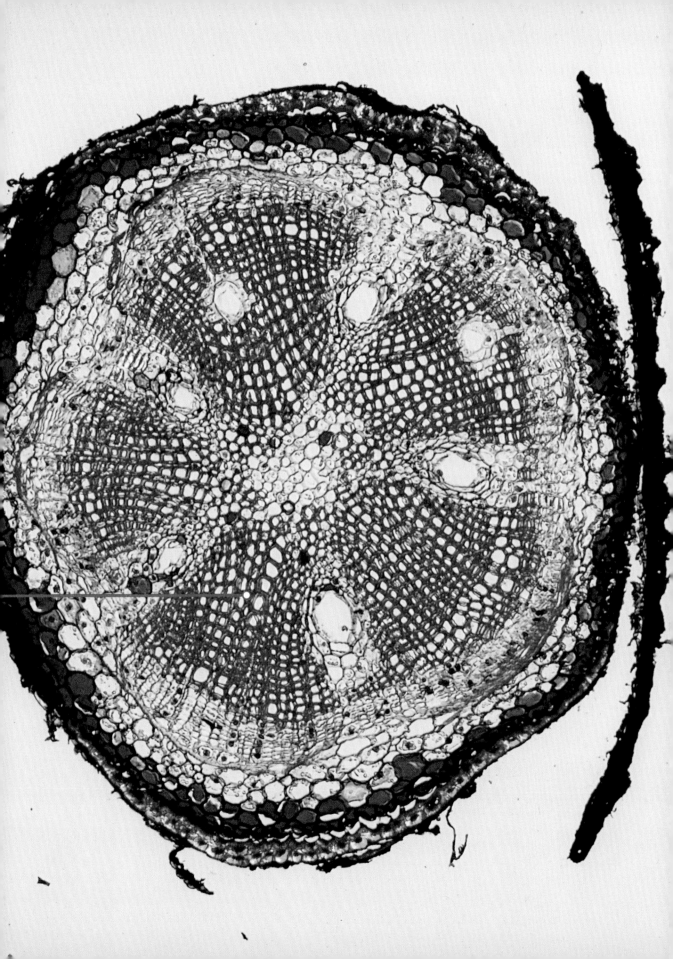

NETWORKING LEAVES

In a leaf, sap flows through a network of veins. Actually, these veins are bundles of tubes. Some tubes carry watery sap into the leaf. The sap is loaded with sugar made by a process called photosynthesis. The sugary sap then flows out through other tubes. The veins are stiffened with a substance called lignin, the tough material that also makes wood strong. When a leaf falls to the ground, the network of veins resists decay much longer than the green cells between the veins.

A network of veins is all that is left of this ivy leaf. The rest of the leaf has decayed — eaten away by organisms that live in huge numbers on the forest floor.

LEAF ART

- It is possible to preserve a leaf skeleton by spreading glue on a sheet of paper and carefully pressing the leaf skeleton on it. After the glue dries, tape the sheet of paper to a window, letting light shine through it.

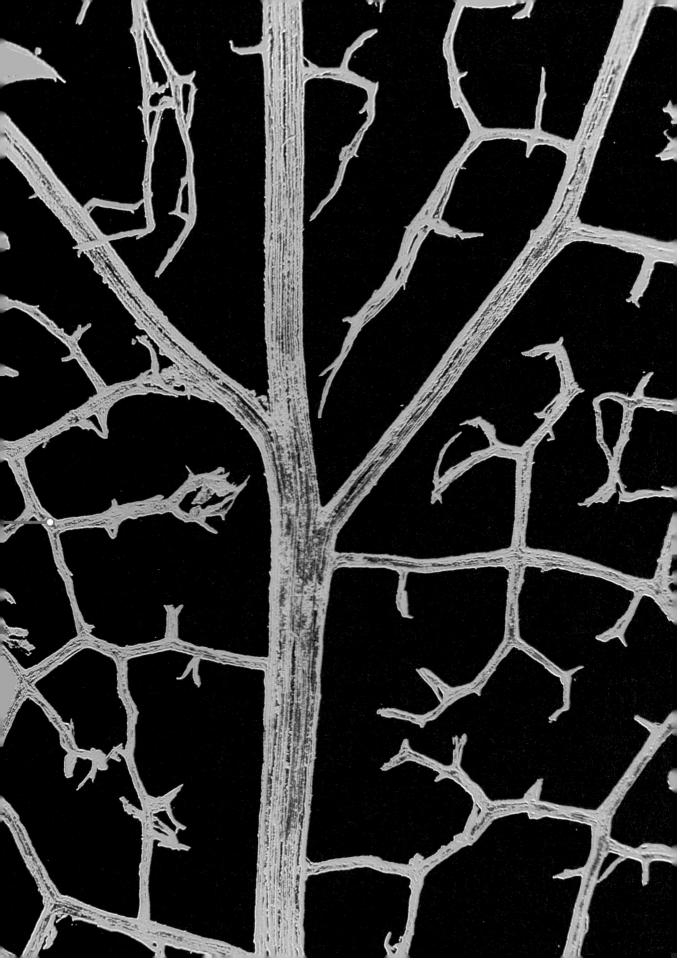

KNOT A PROBLEM

Many pine trees are grown for their lumber. When the trees become large enough, they are cut down, stripped of their bark, and sliced into planks or used as poles. Pine planks always contain numerous round marks, called knots. These are the places where branches had sprouted from the trunk. Sugary sap flowed in from the side branches, while water flowed up from the roots, carried along by chains of tubular cells. The cells were strengthened by a substance known as lignin. These strong cells formed the tough wood of the trunk.

This color-enhanced photo is a slice along the length of a pine trunk. It shows sap-carrying cells *(pink)* swirling around a knot where a branch joins the main trunk.

SOFT, STRONG, AND SPRINGY

- Wood from pine trees is called softwood because it is soft and spongy compared to hardwoods like oak and maple. Pines grow quickly. They are often used in construction because the wood is light and easy to work with, but also strong and springy.

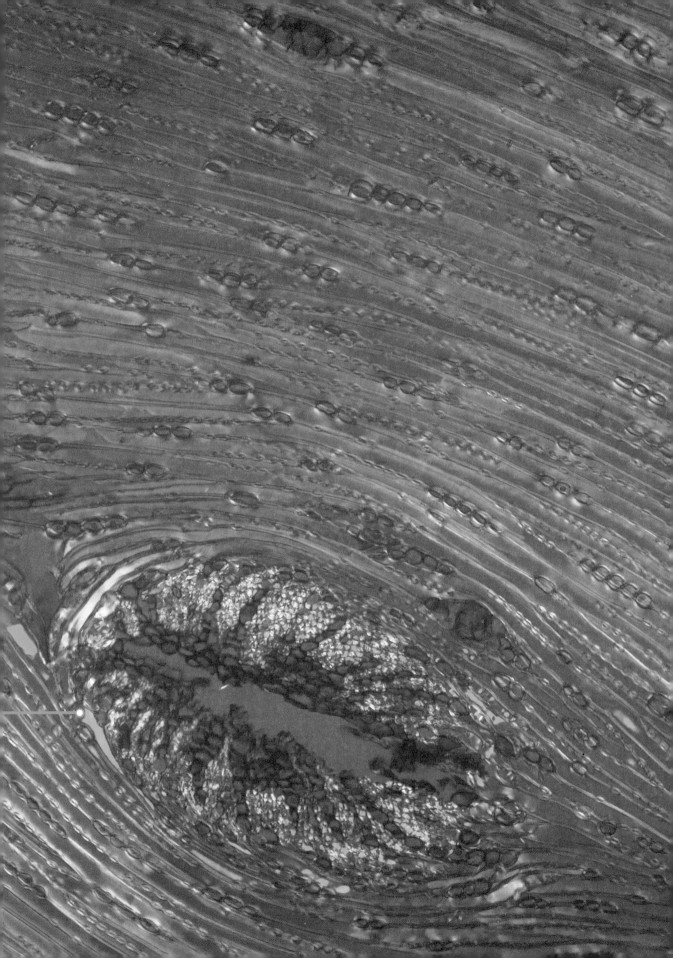

FOREST FERNS

Ferns can only live in damp, shady places. The forest floor is often ideal for them because it is shaded from the sun by leaves of the trees. Ferns develop rows of brown capsules beneath their fronds. In each of the capsules is a package of spores, or seeds. Eventually the packages split open, and the spores blow away on the wind in huge numbers. Any that land in damp, vacant areas have a chance of becoming new ferns, but most of the spores go to waste.

Each of these spore capsules contains many spores. As a capsule dries out, it shrinks. This stretches the capsule wall until it snaps, throwing the spores into the wind.

FERN FRIENDS

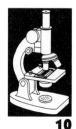

- If you find a fern frond with spore capsules on the underside, tap it over a sheet of paper. If the spores are ripe, they will fall out.
- Tip the spores onto a tray of wet soil. Some may develop into ferns.

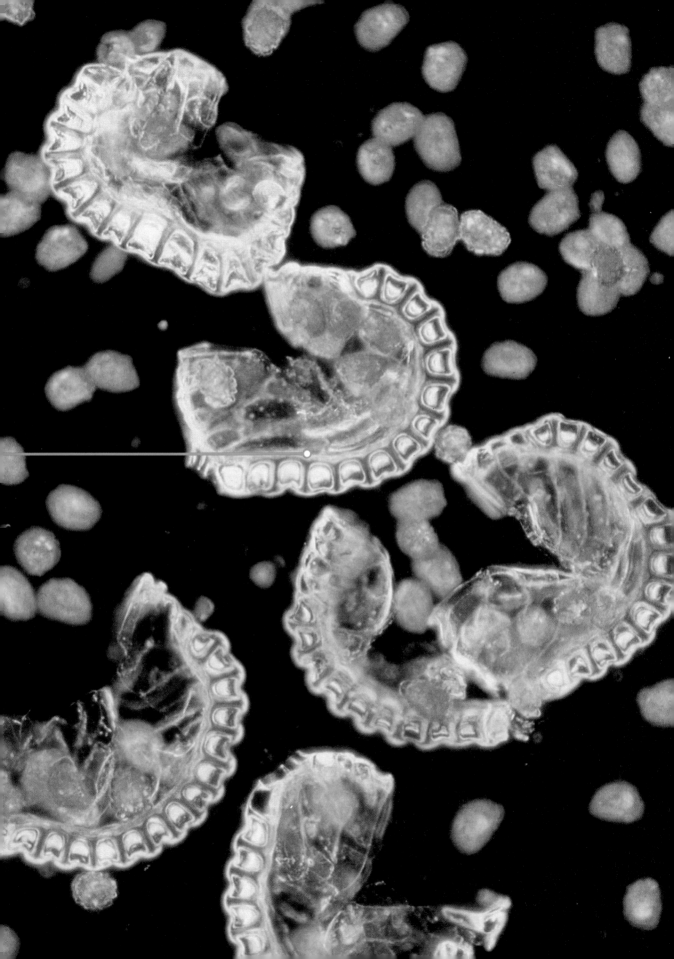

FROM A TINY ACORN

Every giant oak tree began its life as a tiny sapling that sprouted from an acorn. The leaves absorb energy from the sun and use it to make sugar. The sugar is carried throughout the growing tree in the form of sap. It turns into a tough fiber called cellulose. This is the raw material of plant cells that are the "building blocks" of the tree. As the sapling grows, its trunk becomes thicker and gradually develops a strong, woody core. Eventually, the tree spreads into a great dome of beautiful green above the forest floor.

This slice through the stem of a young oak shows the developing wood at its center. The pale dots are tubes that draw water up from the roots to the leaves.

RENEWING THE FOREST

• In the forest, there are tree saplings growing in clearings where old trees have fallen. The newly formed gap in the forest lets light from the sun through, allowing the saplings to grow.

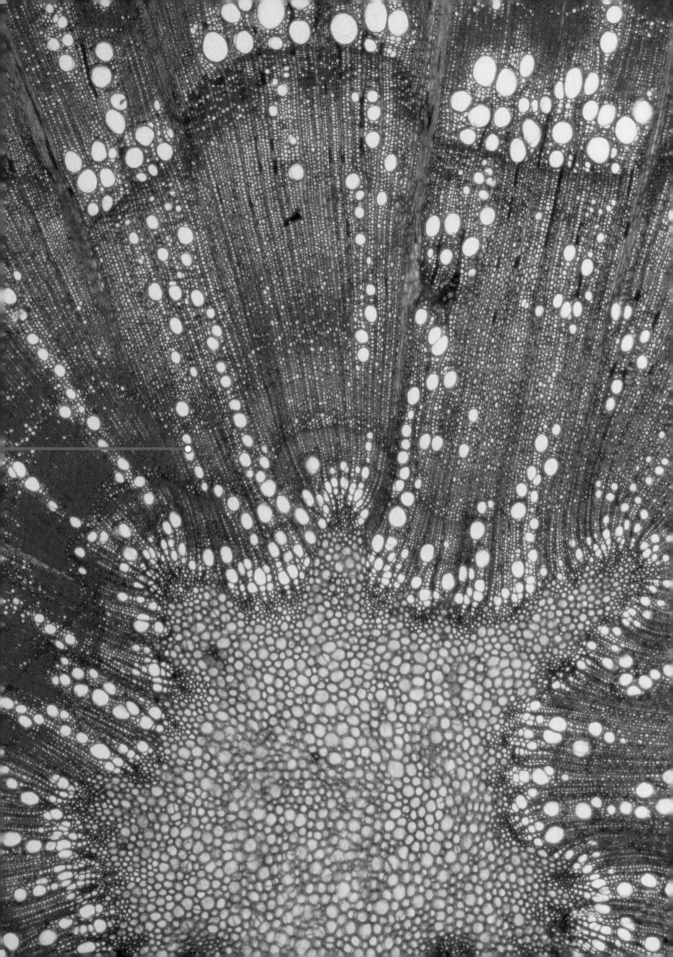

FOREST CARPET

Mosses are soft, cushiony plants that live in damp places. These plants have no roots, so most of them grow close to the ground to keep from drying up. Some mosses, known as sphagnum peat mosses, absorb water like sponges and hold the water in their stems. The mosses often form wet, spongy quilts between the trees in damp forests. Eventually, the ground can become so wet that trees may die. The moss builds up into a dome, with living moss growing on layers of dead moss compressed into peat. These raised areas are called peat bogs.

Sphagnum moss plant cells form networks of long threads. These enclose cavities *(shown in red)* that hold water which mosses need to grow into a thick cushion.

A TRAGIC LOSS

- In many countries, peat moss is gathered and dried to be used as fuel or as compost for plants.
- This demand for peat moss is gradually destroying many peat bogs. This is a tragedy because the bogs are home to many types of rare wildlife.

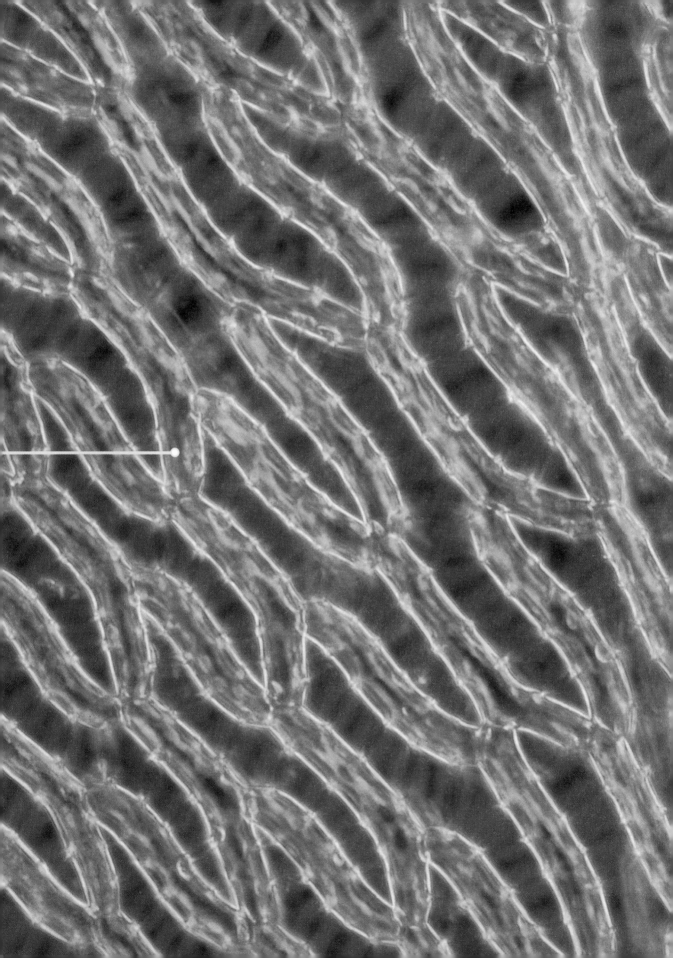

WOODEN HEART

As the stem of a tree transforms into a thick trunk, its core turns into wood. Wood is much tougher than the tissue of a young sapling. The wood is surrounded by a softer layer called bast that carries sugary sap made in the leaves. As the tree gets older, the sap stops flowing through the wood at the core of the trunk. This "heartwood" becomes very hard and solid like a bony skeleton. In very old trees, the core can be destroyed by plants called fungi, which reduce it to powder. The process results in a hollow tree.

This view through the heartwood of an oak tree shows tubes that carry sap throughout the tree. In this photo, the tubes have become blocked by barriers *(yellow)*.

HARD-HEARTED

- In old buildings made with oak beams, the wood is often full of holes drilled by tiny insects called furniture beetles, or woodworms. Yet, oak heartwood is so tough that insects cannot bore into it. Insect damage penetrates only the outer layer.

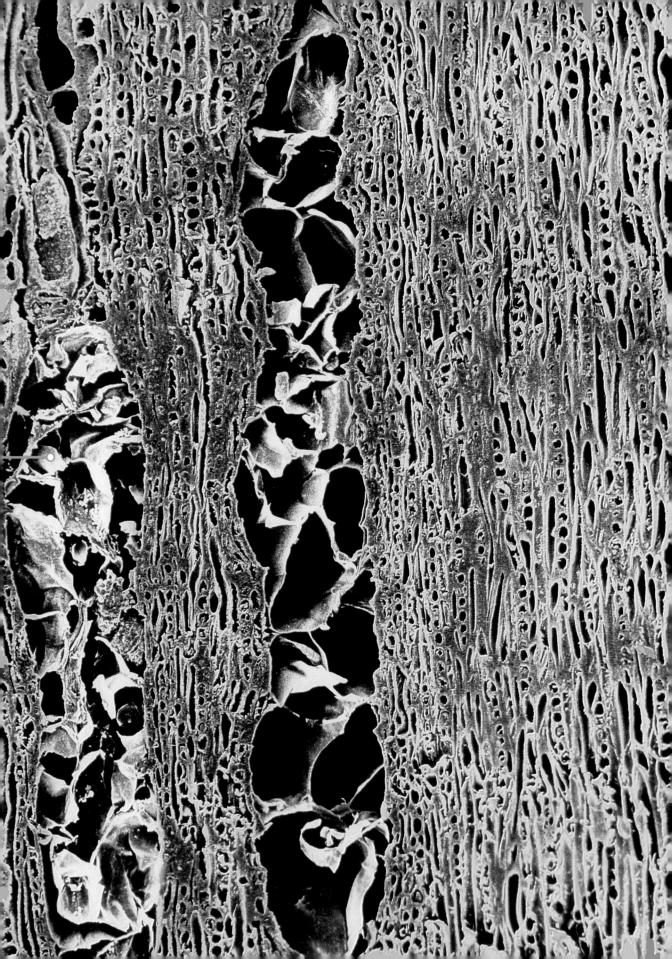

GATHERING MOSS

Fallen trees and stumps in a forest are often covered with mosses — simple green plants that thrive in cool, damp places. All mosses need damp conditions because they do not have the efficient water circulation systems that most green plants have. Each leaf of a moss plant absorbs water from the air. Moss leaves are usually made of a single layer of plant cells joined together like bricks in a path. Each cell contains chlorophyll. This substance absorbs the energy of the sun and uses it to turn carbon dioxide and water into sugar.

Magnified under a microscope, this moss shoot looks like the leaf of a bigger, more advanced plant. Each leaf absorbs the water the plant needs from the air.

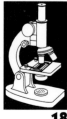

"MOSSIPLICATION"

- Because a moss plant absorbs water and nutrients over its entire surface instead of at the roots, tiny pieces of moss can survive on their own.
- If a moss plant is broken into pieces and kept damp, many of the pieces will grow into new plants.

THICK-SKINNED

The trunk of a tree is covered by a layer of tough bark. Bark keeps the tree from drying out, and it also protects it from injuries caused by insects, large animals, and fires. In addition, bark helps keep out disease. As the tree trunk gets thicker, the bark gets thicker, too. The outer layers of bark are dead. In some trees, the layers peel off, like dead skin. In other trees, the outer layers build up over the years and form a thick corky barrier against damage and decay. The barrier is pierced by small pores that allow the tree to breathe.

This slice through pine bark shows how layers have built up over the years. Eventually the oldest layers peel off, taking diseased spores with them.

BARKING UP A TREE

- Corks that are used to plug bottles are made from the thick bark of a tree called the cork oak.
- Sheets of birch bark were once used by American Indians to make canoes, tepees, and lodges.

TINY VAMPIRES

Bloodsucking parasites called ticks attack animals and even people. A tick must have a lengthy meal of blood before it can breed. Looking like miniature spiders, ticks lurk in the forest. They wait for warm-blooded animals to brush past. A female tick may survive as long as seven years before getting a chance to climb onto a victim, bite through skin, and push a barbed snout into the wound. As the tick feeds on the victim's blood, it steadily inflates until it looks like a shiny, blue pea. When the tick can take no more, it drops off and begins to lay eggs.

The barbed snout of this fear-some deer tick allows it to cling to the skin of a victim. There, it can suck blood for several days without being brushed off.

PERSISTENT PARASITES
- Ticks are extremely difficult to remove from a victim once they have attached themselves.
- Some ticks carry diseases, such as Lyme disease and Rocky Mountain spotted fever, which can be fatal.

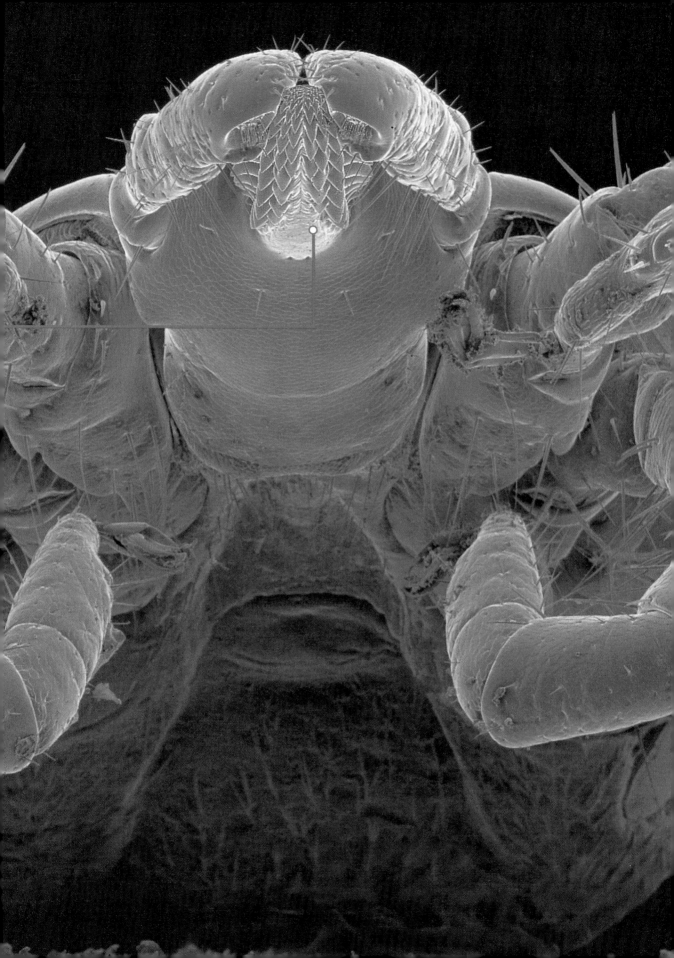

FOOD FACTORY

Leaves of a tree are the tree's food factory. Leaves absorb carbon dioxide from the air and mix it with water drawn up by the roots. They use sunlight to change the mixture into sugar. This process is called photosynthesis. The sugar is dissolved in water and pumped throughout the tree as food. Deciduous trees have broad leaves that absorb as much sunlight as possible. But these leaves also lose a lot of water due to their large surfaces. Trees in dry or cold places, where water is scarce, often have narrow, needlelike leaves. These do not lose a great deal of water.

This specially stained slice through a pine needle, or pine leaf, shows the vessels that carry water into the leaf *(blue)* and carry the sugary sap out *(pink)*.

FALLING LEAVES

• Many broad-leaved trees lose their leaves in the fall. This prevents water loss at a time when water is difficult to get from the cold ground. These trees grow new leaves in spring when water is usually more available.

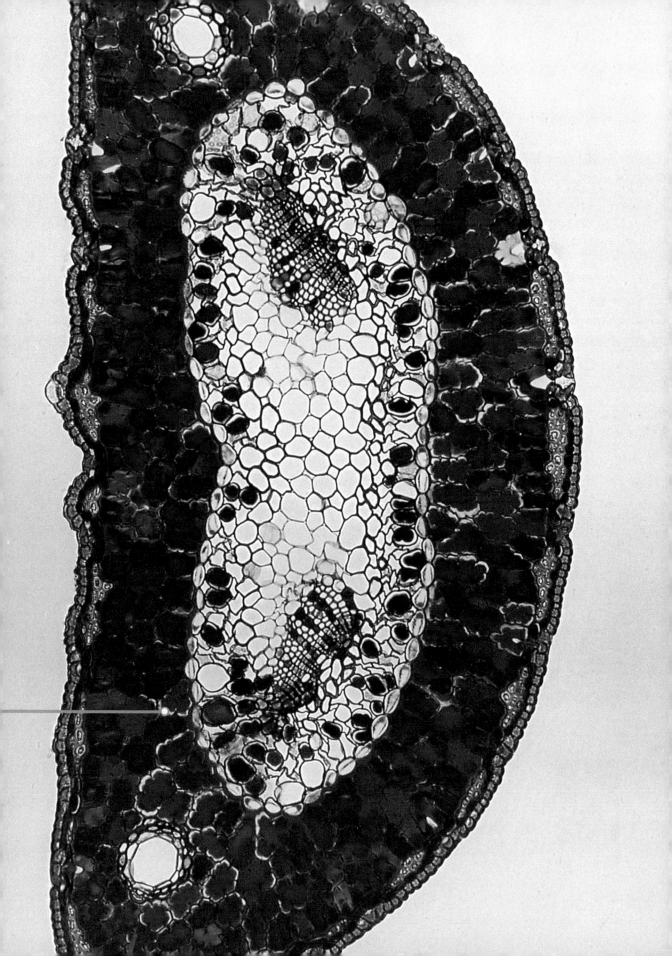

ACID RAINING

A slice through a spruce leaf shows the tree is being destroyed by acid rain. Cells *(top)* have been eaten away, leaving just a few tatters *(bottom)*.

In many parts of the world, forests are being destroyed by a terrible form of pollution known as acid rain. The smoke from factories contains chemicals called oxides. As these oxides blow in the wind, they mix with the droplets of water in clouds, creating acid. Far from the factories that produced the smoke, the acid eventually falls to the ground as acid rain. If the acid rain is absorbed by the leaves of a tree, it eats the leaves away. Finally, the leaves fall off, and the tree may die.

DOWNWIND AND DEADLY

- Acid rain usually affects forests that are downwind from factories. Forests in Canada have been affected by pollution from northern areas of the United States. Scandinavian forests have been almost destroyed by pollution blowing from the United Kingdom, Germany, and Eastern Europe.

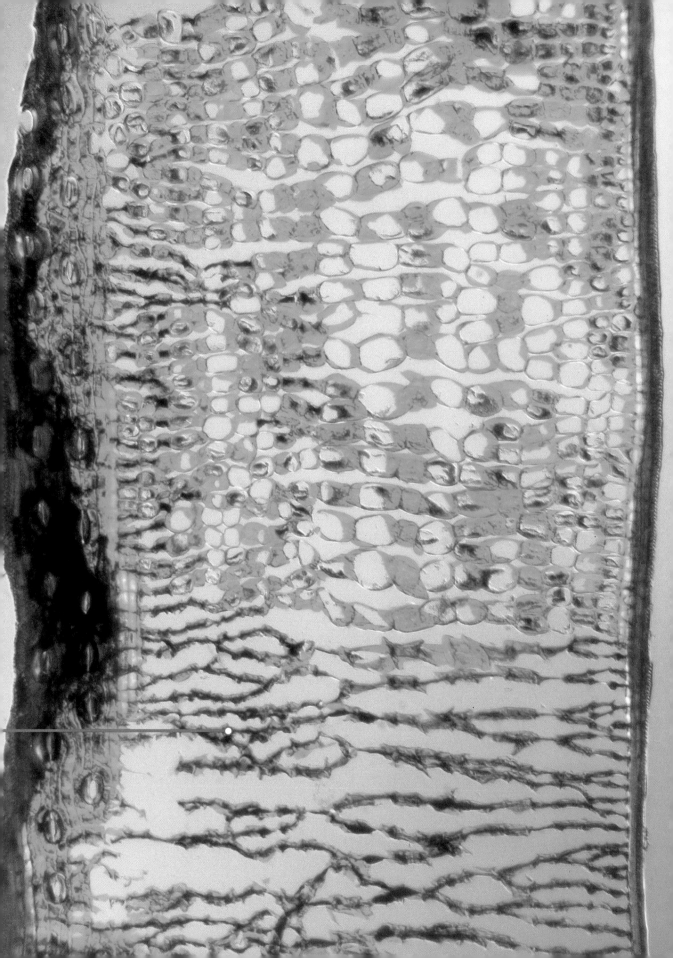

CONIFERS IN THE COLD

The vast dark forests of Canada, Scandinavia, and Siberia are mostly made up of trees called conifers. Conifers have tough, needle-shaped leaves and are better able to survive the cold than trees with broad leaves. Many conifers also have down-sloping branches so that snow easily slides off them. Instead of producing seeds in fruits and nuts, conifers carry seeds in woody cones. The cones of the Norway spruce start out as dark red flowers. The flowers change to green cones and then brown cones. After a year, the cones release their seeds.

A slice across a Norway spruce cone shows the developing seeds. Each tree may produce millions of seeds each year, but only a few grow into new trees.

TOP BILLING

• Some birds, called crossbills, remove seeds from conifers. These special birds have bills that are like crossed fingers. This is the perfect shape for slipping between the scales of the cones to reach the seeds.

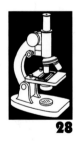

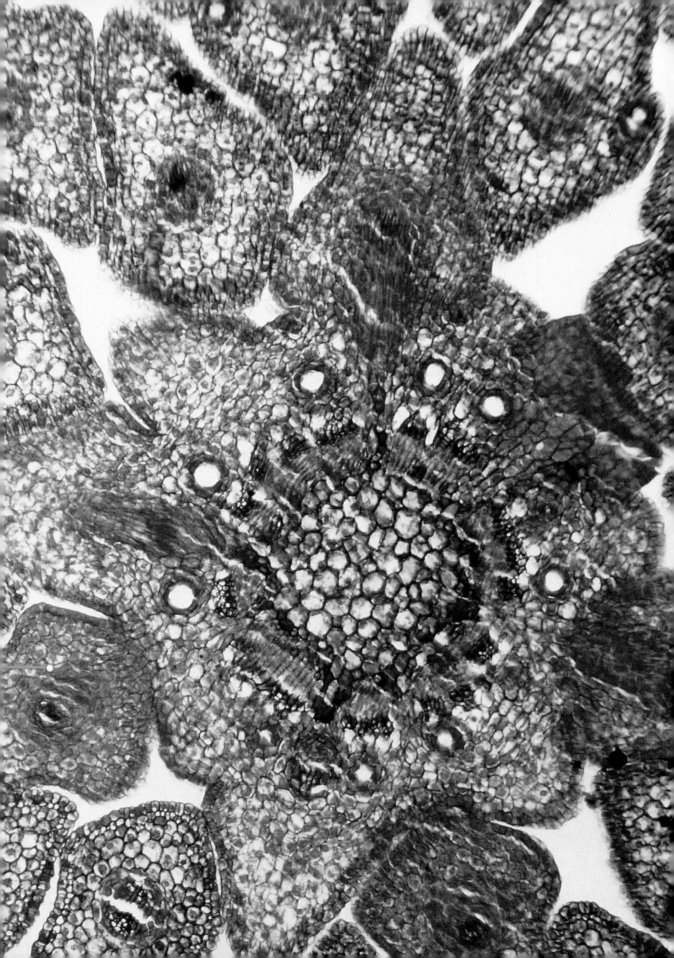

GLOSSARY

bast: the soft layer of wood that can be found just inside the bark of a tree.

cellulose: the tough material that forms the walls of plant cells.

conifers: evergreen trees and shrubs that keep their leaves throughout the year.

deciduous trees: trees that lose their leaves each autumn and grow them back in the spring.

fungi: plants, such as mushrooms, that cannot make food using the sun's energy.

lignin: the substance that strengthens cellulose to make wood.

minerals: natural materials in the soil that are not plant or animal in origin.

organism: an animal or plant of any kind.

oxide: a chemical made by the combination of oxygen with a mineral or gas.

photosynthesis: the conversion of water and carbon dioxide into sugar, using energy from sunlight. This process takes place in the leaves of green plants.

pollution: any substance produced by human activities that poisons the air, water, or landscape.

sap: the sugary fluid inside a tree that is used as food.

spore: the tiny seed of a fern or fungus.

xylem: the tube system in a plant that carries water and minerals.

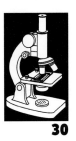

FURTHER STUDY

BOOKS

Ancient Forests. Margaret Anderson, et al (Dog Eared Publications)

Bloodthirsty Plants (series). Victor Gentle (Gareth Stevens)

Eco-Journey (series). Behm/Bonar (Gareth Stevens)

Fungi. Jenny Tesar (Blackbirch)

Mosses. Sylvia Johnson (Lerner)

Why Are the Rain Forests Vanishing? Ask Isaac Asimov (series). Isaac Asimov (Gareth Stevens)

Why Do Leaves Change Color? Betsy Maestro (HarperCollins)

VIDEOS

Biomes (series): Coniferous Forest. Temperate Deciduous Forest. Tropical Rain Forest. (Coronet, The Multimedia Co.)

Microscopes: Making It Big. The Nature of Things series. (Filmmakers Library)

Photosynthesis. (Phoenix/BFA)

Plants: Green, Growing, Giving Life. (Rainbow Educational Video)

What Good Are Woods? Forever Wild (series). (Agency for Instructional Technology)

INDEX